West Germany

Federal Republic of Germany

Editor Chester Fisher
Assistant Editor Dale Gunthorp
Design Patrick Frean
Picture Research Ed Harriman
Production Phillip Hughes
Illustrations John Shackell
Ron Hayward
John Mousdale
Marilyn Day
Eric Jewel
Maps Matthews and Taylor Associates

First published 1974
Macdonald Educational Limited
Holywell House
London, E. C. 2

© Macdonald Educational
Limited 1974

ISBN 0 356 04851 9

Published in the United
States by Silver Burdett
Company, Morristown, N. J.
1976 Printing

Library of Congress
Catalog Card No. 75-44866

West Germany

George Morey

Macdonald Educational

Contents

The beginnings of Germany

The warlike tribes

When Julius Caesar visited the Rhine, German tribes occupied a large part of western and central Europe. Many of them continued to live beyond the Roman Empire, and the Romans were more concerned to prevent them from crossing the Rhine and Danube than in conquering them. Tacitus, the Roman historian, found the Germans uncivilized and warlike, but he admired their strict morals. Germans who lived near the Roman towns learned new skills, and many served in the Roman army.

The Holy Roman Empire

In 800 A.D. Charlemagne joined the tribes together in a great empire which included not only Germany but France and parts of Italy. The rulers who came after him were not such able men, and the differences between one part of Germany and another were very great. Germany became a country made up of hundreds of little, independent States. Charlemagne's Holy Roman Empire continued to exist, and people dreamed of uniting Germany, but there were problems which kept Germany divided. Apart from the North Sea coast and the Baltic, Germany has few natural boundaries. German is the language of many people who live outside Germany, and this has given rise to trouble. Then during the Reformation, a split occured between the Catholic and Protestant princes in Germany.

The German people today

Like other nations, Germany is made up of people of different origins. Hitler foolishly believed that he could make Germany racially "pure". Today, with the foreign workers who have settled, and the refugees from the east, West Germany is even more mixed racially than before.

▲ The remains of Neanderthal Man, who lived 100,000 years ago, were found near Dusseldorf in 1856. He was then thought to be the ancestor of modern man, but much more has since been discovered about the history of the early German peoples.

▲ A prehistoric lake village. A reconstruction built on the site of an actual lake village at Unterhuldingen, Lake Constance.
▼ A Roman commander with German followers. In towns which the Romans built, the Germans quickly adopted Roman ways.

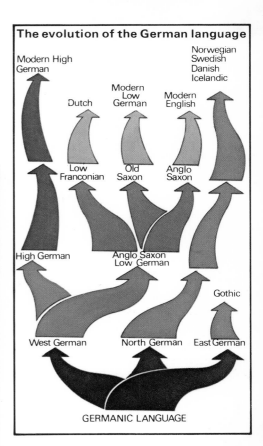

▼ Charlemagne, first Holy Roman Emperor (742-814). He was one of the founders of Western civilization after the fall of Rome. He created a vast, well-governed empire, which included France and part of Italy, as well as Germany. He was not an educated man, but he encouraged learning, and invited many craftsmen and scholars to his Court. He had a palace at Aachen.

The evolution of the German language

Modern High German

Dutch

Modern Low German

Modern English

Norwegian
Swedish
Danish
Icelandic

Low Franconian

Old Saxon

Anglo Saxon

High German

Anglo Saxon Low German

Gothic

West German

North German

East German

GERMANIC LANGUAGE

▲ The German language is closely related to several other West European languages, including English and Dutch.

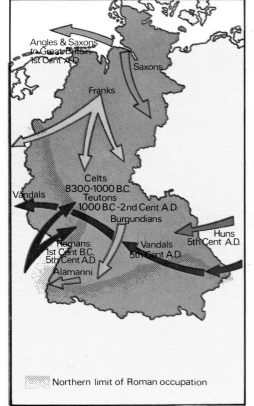

Angles & Saxons to Great Britain 1st Cent A.D.

Saxons

Franks

Celts 8300-1000 B.C. Teutons 1000 B.C -2nd Cent A.D.

Burgundians

Vandals

Romans 1st Cent B.C. 5th Cent A.D.

Alamanni

Vandals 5th Cent A.D.

Huns 5th Cent A.D.

▒ Northern limit of Roman occupation

▲ West Germany's position in the centre of Europe made it a cross-roads in the movement of tribes. These people were driven southwards and westwards.

▼ A young family enjoys a day out together. Though a nation with a venerable history, West Germany has become identified today with youth, energy and industrial progress.

A diverse and beautiful land

The lively regions

Until modern times Germany was divided into hundreds of small states. Many had their own courts, their own governments and armies. This affected the way people thought and behaved, and it still has some influence today. Although the old courts have long been abolished, and there is one West German government, the country is divided up into ten states (*Länder*), which have quite a lot of independence. It often matters much more to politicians what the newspapers in their own state are saying than what appears in the national newspapers.

One good result of this is that, while capital cities have drawn off the best local talent in other countries, this has not happened in Germany. Towns like Cologne, Dusseldorf and Mainz continue to make a vital contribution to national culture. Regional customs and some regional costumes still survive.

Mountains, heaths and cities

Although West Germany is only about as big as the United Kingdom, if offers considerable variety of scenery. The sandy beaches along the North Sea and Baltic and the wide, flat heathland of Lüneburg quickly give way to the central highlands, and further south are the mountains of Bavaria. The smoking factory chimneys of the Ruhr seem a long way from the remote villages and fairy-tale castles of the south.

There are many differences in dress, customs and style of speech between the regions. Since much German humour depends on dialect, a Bavarian joke may not even make a Rhinelander smile!

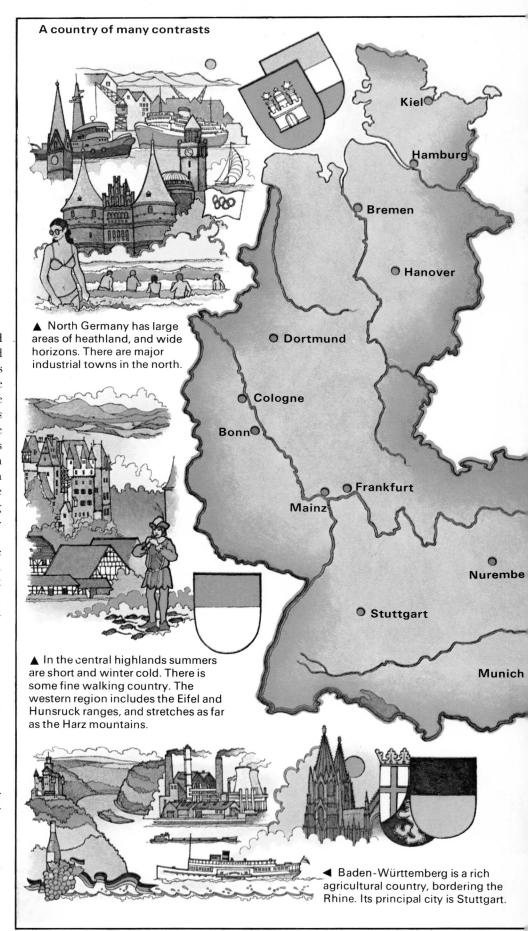

A country of many contrasts

▲ North Germany has large areas of heathland, and wide horizons. There are major industrial towns in the north.

Kiel
Hamburg
Bremen
Hanover
Dortmund
Cologne
Bonn
Frankfurt
Mainz
Nuremberg
Stuttgart
Munich

▲ In the central highlands summers are short and winter cold. There is some fine walking country. The western region includes the Eifel and Hunsruck ranges, and stretches as far as the Harz mountains.

◄ Baden-Württemberg is a rich agricultural country, bordering the Rhine. Its principal city is Stuttgart.

▲ Berlin was the capital of Germany, and is still the largest city. It is divided in two by the Berlin wall, which was erected by the East German authorities.

▲ The panorama of Hamburg docks. Hamburg is the biggest inland seaport in Europe and the most important industrial town in West Germany. The town was badly damaged during the war, but has now been restored and is busier than ever.

▲ Bavaria, with its lakes and alpine scenery is one of the best-known areas. Local costume and some old customs survive.

▼ Preparing the fields on a farm in the Weser valley. In recent years, German agriculture has become much more efficient. Small farms have been joined together to make larger ones, more machinery has been introduced, and farmers have been taught better methods.

How West Germans view each other

▲ To the northerner, the Bavarian seems to take life very easily. He is fond of good living, and speaks a dialect which is not easily understood.

▲ The southerner thinks the northerner is serious and sober. He is considered to be hard working and honest, and what he builds is meant to last.

West Germany and the world

Merchants and artists

It was only at the end of the last century that Germany began to take a place beside Britain and France as a world trader and colonizer. But from early times she was involved in commerce. As a result many Germans became wealthy and important as merchants and bankers. At the same time, the cultures of the outside world were introduced into Germany by these travelling businessmen.

Later, Germany produced some of the world's greatest creative artists. These included musicians like Beethoven, Bach, Brahms and Mendelssohn; writers like Goethe and Schiller, and painters like Hans Holbein. Scientists and thinkers were no less great. Among people who have influenced theories about society and the shape of the universe were Karl Marx and Albert Einstein.

Germans abroad

Sometimes, Germany's influence has been great in spite of herself. In the nineteenth century, thousands left to settle in Britain and the United States because they felt that Germany would never be a free country. After 1933, thousands were forced to leave their homes and their jobs in Germany and the countries where they settled gained a great deal.

Some important Germans

▲ Martin Luther (1483-1546). He was a monk and theologian, and one of the great leaders of the Protestant Reformation. His followers continue to play a vital role in the religious life of the Western world.

▲ Karl Marx (1818-83), the father of communism. He studied the economic forces at work in society and urged that the workers should seize power through revolution.

▲ Albert Einstein (1879-1955). He was one of the greatest physicists who ever lived. He explained in theory certain laws which govern the universe. Recent experiments in space suggest that he was right.

▲ A German force attacked by African tribesmen, 1891. The German Emperor wanted colonies, believing that overseas possessions would make Germany more powerful. He was supported in this by German traders and shipowners. After 1885 Germany joined in the scramble for colonies, competing with France, Britain and Italy, and seized territory in east and south west Africa.

BISMARCK
NORTH DAKOTA

▲ United States town sign with a familiar German name. Many Germans settled in North America at the end of the last century.

Politics of peace

Since the last war, West Germany has contributed towards solving world problems. Long before she became a full member of the United Nations, she had joined many of the special groups, and had given money and expertise to developing countries. In Europe, West Germany has played a large part in the work of NATO and the Common Market. West Germany would like to see Europe move forward to complete unity, but this is still a long way off. Meanwhile, she has been improving relations with the Eastern European countries. Many Germans now accept the separation of East and West Germany as a reality.

▲ Nazi troops invade Austria, March 1938. They were not everywhere as welcome as this propaganda photograph suggests. Fears about German ambitions to conquer Austria and other smaller countries helped to bring about World War II.

▶ A Ghanaian student in a German photographic laboratory. Long before becoming a member of the United Nations, West Germany was giving help to developing nations. One form of aid is through training people in technical subjects. The students can then establish more sophisticated industrial methods in their home countries.

▼ Former West German Chancellor, Willi Brandt, and Russian Premier Kosygin sign the Moscow Treaty, August 12, 1970. Good relations with Eastern Europe play an important part in recent West German policy.

Great German contributions

▲ Many of the world's greatest composers have been Germans. They include Bach, Beethoven, Brahms and Mendelssohn.

▲ Germany has produced some of the world's greatest philosophers. Among them have been Kant, Hegel and Schopenhauer.

The family at home

Finding somewhere to live

For many West Germans it has been a hard struggle to get a home of their own because so many houses were destroyed during the War.

There are now many new flats. Because housing is very expensive, flats are often rather small, and many have no garden at all. People make the best of it by buying furniture which serves more than one purpose.

Since there are few gardens in the towns, Germans spend a lot on indoor plants and, in smaller towns, it is often possible to hire a plot on the outskirts where flowers can be grown. Nowadays only rich people can afford servants, but it is usually possible to get a daily help who will come in for an hour. For the rest, the family has to help itself, especially if the mother goes to work.

Inside the block

Few German flats have caretakers, and people on each floor take turns to keep the passages and stairs clean. Little notices on the walls show whose turn it is, and who is to blame if the work is not well done.

Sunday afternoon is the time to expect guests, but in case an unexpected visitor arrives, the living room is kept neat and tidy at all times.

In the home, the furniture is likely to be very modern and light, or heavy and dark—both extremes are popular. The old-fashioned tiled stove is not so common now. Today Germans rely very much on central heating. Since winters are often cold in West Germany, and since many Germans like to keep their houses rather warm, windows are usually double glazed.

▲ A modern German house. It has an unusually large and attractive garden.

An average family budget

35·3% Food and fine foods

15·5% Rent

10·8% Clothing and footwear

10·8% Fares etc.

9·0% Household goods

7·3% Education and entertainment

4·7% Fuel, gas and electricity

3·6% Cosmetics etc.

3·0% Personal outlay

▲ This is the way in which the average middle income family of four spent its money in 1971. West Germans then spent over 35 per cent of their income on food which was quite a lot more than the French did! Rent, fares and clothing also took a large part of the family income. Since then prices have shot up, and workers are beginning to demand higher wages.

◀ German children doing their homework. In West Germany there is often no school in the afternoon, but even very young children are given a lot of homework to do. If children are to make good progress later on, it is important to get good marks, and not be obliged to repeat a class. And so parents who want to see their children go to university see that homework is well done.

▲ Preparing a meal. Kitchens are often small, but are modern and well-equipped.

▲ The children's bedroom in a German flat. Bunk beds are common. Most modern flats are small, and it is necessary to make the best use of space.

▼ One of the main shopping streets in Frankfurt. The big stores are as fine as any in Europe.

A typical daily timetable

7.00   **7.45**

11.00

1.00-2.00

2.00-5.00

6.00-7.00

7.30   **8.00-10.00**

A sporting nation

The Munich Olympics

The choice of Munich for the Olympic Games in 1972, and for the World Football Cup in 1974, recognized Germany's place as a leading sporting nation.

People in West Germany take a great interest in sport. No fewer than ten million people are members of the German Sports Union—although not all of them take an active part. There are also many thousands who watch their teams, and follow them when they play abroad. And there are thousands of Germans who go to the winter sports centres for their holidays and at weekends.

The most popular sports are football, gymnastics, athletics, ice-skating, riding and swimming. The names of the great stars in these fields, such as Franz Beckenbauer, Uwe Seeler, Heidi Rosendahl and Hans Winkler are well known, and their performances closely watched. Sports magazines have a considerable number of readers.

Taking part in sports

Many people in West Germany think that sport should have a more important place at school, and that the government should build more centres and swimming pools. Germany has fewer facilities for sport than one would expect from an affluent, health-conscious nation. However, few fans would want sport to be organized by the government as it is in East Germany. Many people have said that they would like to take part if they had the chance. This helps to explain the popularity of sports which call for little organization, such as shooting, bowling, cycling and mountaineering.

▲ Germans support their football internationals with enthusiasm—and have the same habit of invading the pitch.

▼ Ulrike Meyforth, women's high jump champion. At the Munich Olympic games she won the gold medal with a jump of 1.92 metres (6ft 3½in).

▲ The West German champion weightlifter, R. Mang. He won the silver medal in the super-heavyweight class at the Munich Olympics.

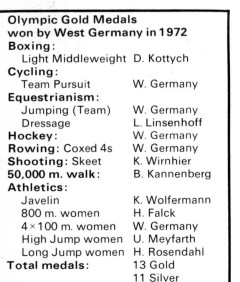

Olympic Gold Medals won by West Germany in 1972	
Boxing:	
Light Middleweight	D. Kottych
Cycling:	
Team Pursuit	W. Germany
Equestrianism:	
Jumping (Team)	W. Germany
Dressage	L. Linsenhoff
Hockey:	W. Germany
Rowing: Coxed 4s	W. Germany
Shooting: Skeet	K. Wirnhier
50,000 m. walk:	B. Kannenberg
Athletics:	
Javelin	K. Wolfermann
800 m. women	H. Falck
4×100 m. women	W. Germany
High Jump women	U. Meyfarth
Long Jump women	H. Rosendahl
Total medals:	13 Gold
	11 Silver
	16 Bronze

Famous West German sportsmen

▲ Gerd Müller, the brilliant West German striker. West Germany won the World Cup in the 1974 games in Mexico.

▲ Hans Winkler, the German horseman. He is known to television viewers for his brilliant performance in competitions.

▲ Klaus Wolfermann. He won the javelin event at the Munich Olympics in 1972 with a magnificent throw of 90.48 metres.

▲ Heidi Rosendahl won the women's long jump at the 1972 Olympics. She was one of the most popular competitors.

▲ Skiing in the Bavarian Alps. Here are some of the best ski runs in the world.

◄ The start of an amateur cycling race at Biberach. In recent years, cycling has become an increasingly popular sport in West Germany.

High standards in education

Many Germans feel that the school system is old-fashioned, and look for improvements. They want many more university places and better further education courses.

High standards

Germans take education very seriously, and high standards are expected. At the moment, the government is finding it hard to provide all the places wanted—especially at nursery schools and universities. Many people think German education is old-fashioned, and changes are now beginning to take place.

At the age of six, nearly every German child goes to the ordinary state school. The first day at school is something every child remembers. Before setting out, each one receives a cone made of cardboard and fancy paper, and filled with sweets and toys. They share these with other children in the class.

After that, work begins in earnest. Children stay at school until they are sixteen, and often much older.

The school day

Most schools start at 8 o'clock and lessons go on until 1 o'clock. There is at least one break (when pupils can eat their second breakfast). There is often no afternoon school, but even quite young children get lots of homework. For many there is school on Saturday mornings too.

For many parents, the school years are an anxious time. German parents are often ambitious for their children. They want them to succeed well at school and go to university, for university graduates have high social status and access to better jobs. So fathers will often pore over the homework, and school reports will be carefully scrutinized.

There are very few comprehensive schools in Germany at present, and most pupils go to separate academic or technical secondary schools.

▲ A chemistry lesson in a West German school. The master and senior pupils are working on a petroleum distillation experiment. To a much greater extent than in other countries, the grammar schools specialize. Pupils, at their choice, concentrate upon classics, modern languages or mathematics and science.

▼ The end of the school day in a junior school. Even young children use shoulder satchels or carry briefcases for their books and homework. This school dates from before the war, but in the big towns many were destroyed and had to be rebuilt. The opportunity has been taken to build modern classrooms and gymnasiums.

▲ The **secondary school** provides education for most German children till 16. They then work and go to school part-time until age 18.

▲ The **grammar school** (*Gymnasium*) provides a nine-year course. There are separate schools for science, languages and classics.

▲ Pupils who pass the *Abitur* may apply for places in the 25 **universities**. It has been difficult to find places for them all.

▲ There are not enough **nursery schools**. Only one child in three finds a place. There are no formal lessons.

▲ Nearly every German child goes to a **primary school** from six to ten years. There are very few private schools.

▲ The **Mittelschule** provides a six-year course leading to about O-levels for those entering business or industry.

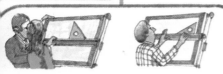

▲ The **Aufbauschule** provides a more advanced technical instruction for some of the pupils of the *Mittelschule*.

▲ A classroom in a Munich school. After the war many schools had to be rebuilt, and the opportunity was taken to introduce modern equipment. At the same time a lot of thought is being given to changing the whole school system to meet needs of the present day.

▶ Students at work in a university library. German students are expected to cover large syllabuses and to work hard. The demand for places at the universities has been so great that there is much overcrowding.

▼ A gymnasium in a modern German school. The newly-built schools are much better equipped with facilities for physical training. The arrangement of the school day, which ends very early in the afternoon, makes it difficult to fit physical training and sport into the curriculum.

Getting away from it all

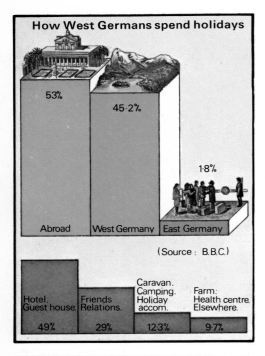

How West Germans spend holidays

53%	45.2%	1.8%
Abroad	West Germany	East Germany

(Source : B.B.C.)

Hotel. Guest house.	Friends. Relations.	Caravan. Camping. Holiday accom.	Farm: Health centre. Elsewhere.
49%	29%	12.3%	9.7%

Great travellers

West Germans have more holidays and shorter working hours than people in Britain or France. They also have more money to spend than ever before, and it is again possible for them to travel abroad freely.

Millions of Germans take their holidays abroad. Italy, Spain, Yugoslavia and Greece are particular favourites, but groups of travellers are to be met in far distant countries. Many Germans have even bought holiday homes for themselves in foreign countries, but this is more difficult now.

Holidays at home

Others find that their own country, as well as Austria and Switzerland, gives them opportunities for outdoor holidays. Walking and climbing, swimming and fishing, and sightseeing are popular. The sandy beaches on the North Sea and the Baltic are also good for home holidays. Germany was the first country to provide youth hostels so that young people could travel around their country cheaply. These hostels, often in interesting old buildings, are very well run.

Many Germans take two holidays: perhaps a visit abroad, and a short holiday at home.

▲ A seaside resort on the Baltic coast. The clean sandy beaches and the sunshine make them especially popular for holidays. A fresh breeze sometimes makes it necessary to dig oneself a sun-trap in the sand as these people have done.

◄ A holiday village in the Bavarian Alps. Nearly 3.5 million West Germans go skiing every winter. In the country around such villages even beginners can find easy runs.

▼ West Germany's 1,300 camping sites are carefully graded, and well organized. Many are attractively situated, with arrangements for cars.

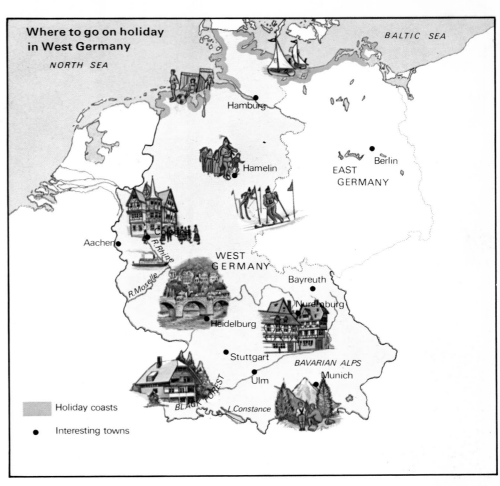

Where to go on holiday in West Germany

NORTH SEA

BALTIC SEA

Hamburg

Hamelin

Berlin

EAST GERMANY

Aachen

Cologne

R.Rhine

R.Moselle

WEST GERMANY

Bayreuth

Nuremburg

Heidelburg

Stuttgart

BAVARIAN ALPS

Ulm

Munich

BLACK FOREST

L.Constance

Holiday coasts

Interesting towns

▲ The Germans are well aware of the beauty and historical interest of their country, and take care to preserve it and make it known. West Germany is a country which has something to offer everybody whether they are looking for a quiet holiday or an opportunity for exercise.

▼ A man on a hike. Many Germans are fond of long country walks. To help them, many communities mark the best walks with coloured signs on posts and trees, and publish details about them. In the mountains distances are shown in the length of time it takes to walk to a place.

Tradition and superstition

Days for making merry

Hundreds of festivals take place in Germany every year. Nearly every village has its saint's day and, especially in Catholic districts, these are occasions for merry-making. The festivals before the beginning of Lent at Cologne, Mainz and Munich are world-famous. The most important events take place just before Ash Wednesday, but as early as the previous November the first of the meetings and parties are being held to raise money, and discuss plans for the processions and dances. Germans find it a great opportunity to let off steam, by going about the town in fancy dress, and by poking fun at the town officials. Carnival-time is less popular with young Germans than it once was.

Everywhere in Germany, Easter and Christmas are especially important. By tradition Easter is the time of the Easter rabbit, who hides coloured eggs about the house.

Christmas festivities

Many Christmas customs—including the lighted Christmas tree, Christmas stories and carols, have a German origin. For Germans Christmas begins early (on December 6, St Nicholas's Day) and goes on until Twelfth Night. On Christmas Eve, the Christmas tree is lit, and everyone joins in singing carols. The family often goes to church in the evening, and everyone pretends to be surprised to find the presents which Santa Claus has left round the tree while they have been in church. Christmas Day is by contrast, fairly quiet, and a time for visiting friends.

In southern Germany especially, Christmas ends with the festival of the Three Kings. The letters C.M.B.—the initials of the Three Kings—are to be seen chalked on front doors, and children, dressed as the Three Kings go from house to house, singing carols.

▲ Every year the story of the Pied Piper is performed in the streets of Hamelin, with the participants in fancy dress. Nowadays, the children and the "rats" always return!

Some German customs

▲ People shake hands much more frequently in Germany than they do in most other places.

▲ An ancient inn-sign. Beautiful examples of the metalworkers' craft are to be found in many places. These indicated the name of the house or the trade that was carried on.

▲ Dogs are a privileged class in Germany, and are taken where they would not be admitted elsewhere.

▲ At the new year, people melt a piece of lead in an old spoon, and tip it into a basin of water. They try to read their fortune from the shapes formed by the solidifying lead.

▲ A big paper cone of sweets is given to small children when they first go to school.

▲ In Germany it is considered polite for gentlemen to walk on the left-hand side. This can cause problems in muddy streets!

▼ Being the first to hear the cuckoo in spring is always a sign of good fortune. If one does not hear a cuckoo, one has at least had a good spring walk.

▼ A Bavarian village band. Nearly every important village has its own band, which plays at weekends.

▲ A decorated maypole in a Munich street. Such May Day celebrations have survived from the distant past.

Small shops to hypermarkets

Cleanliness and quality

Visitors are always impressed by the fine shops and markets to be found even in small towns. Germans not only want fair prices, they insist that everything be perfectly clean. They like to buy fresh food every day. The baker is often open in time for new rolls for breakfast. Milk is not delivered to the house, but has to be fetched from a nearby dairy.

The small grocery store, crammed with every kind of food, still exists, but thousands close every year as things get difficult for small traders. Many are trying to save money with self-service and by forming co-operatives. In this way they can reduce prices, but even the supermarkets are finding competition hard.

Hypermarkets and warehouses

Two new kinds of store have developed in some big towns. One is the hypermarket. One, near Frankfurt, containing several supermarkets and specialized stores, is said to be the biggest in Europe. There is parking for 5,000 cars. The other kind of store is really a warehouse, where customers help themselves from the cases in which the goods arrived. Both offer bargains.

Many Germans, however, like the little shops, even if it means a rush to get to them during the lunch-hour or while they are open in the evening. The government has now made a small concession to busy working people: shops are allowed to stay open later on the first Saturday of the month.

How some things are sold

▲ An old-fashioned butcher's shop. Only the prices are not old-fashioned! In the past, Germans have been great meat-eaters, and traditional German foods are largely based on pork or beef. Lately, rising prices of meat have somewhat affected this preference.

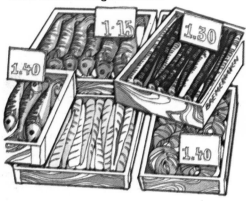

▲ Smoked and pickled fish are German specialities. They are sold in delicatessen stores and can be bought, ready to eat, from stalls at markets and fairs.

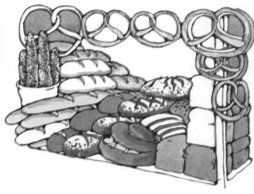

▲ Bread shops sell bread in many different shapes, and of many different kinds. Germans do not seem to be very fond of sliced, wrapped bread!

▲ In West Germany milk must be fetched from the shop. Some supermarkets sell milk in plastic containers, but most housewives go once or twice a day to a dairy produce store.

▲ Open-air vegetable markets are very common in Germany. Farmers often bring their produce directly from the country. Germans like to buy their food fresh daily.

Some West German coins and notes. One Deutschmark (DM) is worth 100 Pfennige —about 17 British pence or 39 American cents.

The many types of sausage and pork

▲ *Blutzungenwurst*, a very popular sausage, made with tongue and pork meat.

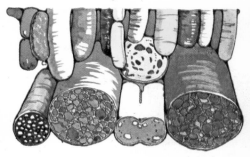

▲ Smoked meats, especially pork, are popular all over Germany. But the home of this rich dish was originally the North.

▲ German sausages exist in dozens of varieties. All are subtly different in taste and take many forms. According to type, they are eaten sliced, spread, poached or fried. They vary from the delicate *Weisswürste* made with veal to *Getrüffelte Gänseleberwurst,* goose-liver sausage flavoured with truffles.

▲ A modern shopping-precinct, Munich. Destruction in Munich during the war made it possible to lay out this traffic-free zone in the middle of the city, with its modern department stores and cafes. Only delivery vehicles are allowed in the mall, so shopping is a pleasure. At the bottom of the picture, steps lead down to a station on Munich's splendid metropolitan railway.

► A modern delicatessen. Such shops can often be found in quite small places. They provide a wonderful range of prepared foods so that it is easy to arrange a quick meal. The standard of cleanliness in such shops is very high indeed.

Eating the German way

Make yourself a German meal

Breakfast: 7.00 a.m. Rolls, butter or jam. Coffee or chocolate. Eggs on Sunday.

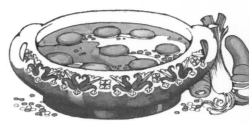

Second breakfast: 10.00-11.00 a.m. Meat or cheese sandwich. Milk.

LINSENSUPPE
½ lb of dried quick-cooking lentils
1½ pts cold water
2 oz lean bacon in one piece
Leek, carrot, parsnip, celery, chopped
½ oz bacon fat

Eating well

West Germany is not so famous as France for the excellence of its cooking skills, but ordinary people can eat better in Germany for the same amount of money than almost anywhere in the world. Thousands of little restaurants and inns pride themselves upon serving first-rate food in pleasant conditions.

Food fashions are changing. Most regions have their own special dishes, and some of these have become world famous. Pork is especially popular, closely followed by beef and veal. Mutton and lamb are not eaten quite so much. As Germany becomes richer, people eat less bread and potatoes, but many more eggs. Supplies from abroad also make dishes more exciting. Germans have always been large eaters, and it is not surprising that being over-weight is a problem. Most Germans eat a very light breakfast, but they take a second breakfast with them to eat later.

Canteen lunches

Nowadays many people travel long distances to work, and many housewives work. Many firms have, therefore, found it necessary to provide canteens. This has changed eating habits, and many families now have two hot meals a day.

For most Germans, however, the main meal is eaten at midday. In some places, work stops for up to two hours. Supper is then a much lighter meal with perhaps just soup and cold meat or sausage on open sandwiches.

Beer is the great national drink and huge quantities are drunk. There are also many fine German wines. The two great wine producing areas follow the course of the two great rivers, the Rhine and the Mosel. Of the two, the wines of the Mosel tend to be lighter and drier.

Lunch: 12.00-2.00 p.m. Salt ribs of pork, pease pudding, boiled potatoes. Apple puree. Beer or fruit juice. On Sundays, a bigger meal.

HIMMEL UND ERDE
(Heaven and earth)
3 fair sized potatoes
1 cooking apple, sliced
Small onion, sliced into rings
3 oz lean bacon, diced
½ pt water; salt, pepper and sugar

Supper: 7.30 p.m. Open sandwiches of sliced meat, sausage and cheese. Salad and fruit. Beer or fruit juice.

ST. GERVAIS IN PFIRSICH
Half a peach per person
St. Gervais cream cheese
Cocktail cherry

Wash the lentils thoroughly. Bring the water to the boil and add the lentils, bacon and vegetables (except the onion) and simmer for 30 minutes. Melt the bacon fat, add the onion and cook till soft. Add a little flour and stir till flour turns golden. Tip onions into lentil soup and simmer for about 30 minutes until lentils are tender but not mushy. Before serving cut bacon into small pieces and add one or two frankfurter sausages cut into thin slices. Taste to see whether a little salt or black pepper is needed.

Put the sugar, a little salt and pepper into a saucepan with the water. Add the potatoes and apple, bring to the boil, and simmer until the potatoes are tender but not falling apart. Meanwhile cook the bacon in a pan. When ready, drain it on a layer of kitchen paper, and cook onions gently in the fat.

Check the potatoes, if necessary add a little salt, and then pour everything into a heated bowl. It is very nice eaten with crisply cooked black pudding. But remember to skin the black pudding.

Arrange the peach-halves (either fresh or tinned according to season) together with a little fruit juice in individual bowls. Fill the peaches with St. Gervais cheese and top with a cocktail cherry. It is usual to pour a little kirsch over the sweet at the moment of serving, and to light it with a match, but this is of course optional!

▲ A restaurant interior. Germans set great store by comfortable surroundings and good service. There are thousands of such old inns providing good food and wine.

Famous regional dishes

Rollmops
▲ Salted herring fillets, prepared with spices, onions and gherkins and soaked in brine. They are a speciality of Berlin and the North Sea coast.

Kalbshaxe
▲ Baked knuckle of veal (*Kalbshaxe*) is the national dish of Bavaria. It is lightly salted and roasted, then served in a rich gravy. It is eaten with mixed salad.

▲ Westphalian ham, a speciality of central Germany. Served with gherkins and pumpernickel bread, it makes a traditional breakfast.

◄ The midday meal. Father has his lunch at the factory or the office, while mother and the children eat at home when school is over for the day.

Roulade
▲ This Rhineland dish is made with strips of rump steak filled with bacon, onions and pickled cucumber. It is often eaten with hot boiled red cabbage and delicious "fluffy" dumplings.

Black Forest Cherry Cake
▲ This is made with layers of chocolate sponge, spread with black cherry jam, soft cherries and whipped cream. The finished cake is covered with flaked chocolate.

29

The vital place of the arts

Importance of the arts

The arts, especially music and the theatre, play an important part in the lives of German people. Even quite small towns support theatres where plays, ballets and concerts are performed through most of the year. There are nearly 80 symphony orchestras, some internationally known.

The festivals at Bayreuth, Würzburg, Bonn and Wiesbaden were re-established after the war and now attract artists and audiences from all over the world. Every ten years, the Bavarian mountain-village of Oberammergau presents a play based on the life and death of Christ.

Many German people, however, are not content to listen to music and look at the work of others. They like to perform, write and paint. Germany is well-provided with amateur societies and schools where they can practise and study.

Recovery after the war

At first, after the war, it seemed strange to West Germans to be allowed to express themselves without fear of the government. Much of the early writing, therefore, was done by people returning from abroad. Now there are again many men and women who are making names for themselves. Germany is among the world-leaders in the number of books published.

Early German films had won wide respect, but after the war film-making was hampered because most of the studios were in East Berlin.

◄ "The Knight, Death and the Devil", an engraving by Dürer. Albrecht Dürer (1471-1528) was one of Germany's greatest artists.

Scene from Wagner's opera *Tannhäuser*. Richard Wagner (1813-83) frequently used the legends of Germany's pagan past for the plots of his operas.

▲ Klee's stage setting for the opera, *Sinbad the Sailor*. Paul Klee (1879-1940), who was Swiss by birth, did much of his work as a painter and teacher in Germany.

◄Ludwig van Beethoven (1770-1827), one of the most famous of all German composers. He was born in Bonn. He composed sonatas, quartets, symphonies and the opera *Fidelio*. He lost his hearing later in life, but continued to compose, even though he could only ''hear'' this music in his mind.

▲ A scene from Bertolt Brecht's play, *Mother Courage,* a chronicle play about the Thirty Years War. Brecht's best-known play is the *Threepenny Opera*. His realistic style and concern for the sufferings of the poor have greatly influenced playwrights in the present day.

◄ Faust signs a blood pact with the devil in a scene from Goethe's play. Faust sought youth and power in exchange for his soul. The story of Faust, or Dr. Faustus, has been retold in many languages.

A genius for invention

The invention of printing

The German invention which has been of the greatest benefit was probably the invention of printing. Printing of sorts—in which the design was carved on a block of wood—had been used for a long time to make things like playing-cards. But before books could be printed, it was necessary to invent a system using separate letters, which could be locked together to form the words of the page, and then taken apart for another page. At the time people in many countries were trying to find a way to produce cheap books, but Gutenburg was the first in Europe to find an answer.

Among the earliest of Germany's famous scientists was Kepler, the great astronomer. More famous was Rontegen, who discovered X-rays, and Professors Erlich and Koch, who did important work on serious diseases. Much more recently, the rocket engineer, von Braun, has advanced space research.

Science in daily life

The work of scientists is often hard to understand. As a result, Professor Bunsen is better known for the Bunsen burner, which is used in every chemistry classroom, than for the other important work which he did!

German firms have given a lead to modern research by hiring scientists to work together as a team to solve problems which concerned the firm.

▼ Johann Gutenberg (1397-1468), the inventor of modern printing, was born and died in Mainz. In spite of his great skill, he was not a good businessman and died in poverty.

Schliemann—discoverer of Troy

▲ Heinrich Schliemann (1822-90). His discoveries at Troy and Mycenae created a great sensation and put archaeology on a new course.

▲ Schliemann's wife, wearing some of the priceless jewels discovered in Greece and Asia Minor.

corde: qm̄ ipī dm̄ uidebūt. Beati pa-
cifici: qm̄ filii dei uocabūtur. Beati q̄
plecucionē patiūtur ꝓpter iusticiam:
qm̄ ipsoꝝ est regnū cloꝝ. Beati estis
cū maledixerint uobis·et plecuti uos
fuerint et dixerūt oīe malū aduersū
uos mētientes ꝓpter me. Gaudete ⁊

▲ Gutenberg's printing press. The big screw and lever pressed the paper firmly onto the inked type-bed. What made Gutenberg's press better than any earlier press was that he had found a way of making "movable type", so that the letters could be used over and over again to make up fresh words after each page had been printed.

◄ An extract from Gutenberg's Bible.

The father of the motor car

◄ Karl Benz (1844-1929) is credited with making the first practical motor-car in 1885, although several other inventors were working on similar lines at the same time. Gottlieb Daimler was a near neighbour, but the two men never met, although their firms later amalgamated.

▼ Benz's first car was a two-seater, three-wheel vehicle, with wire wheels and solid tyres. The motor was placed over the rear driving-axle. It had an output of 1½ h.p. The front wheel was steered by a short hand-lever. Two motor cars were made to this design in 1885. It had a top speed of 7 miles per hour.

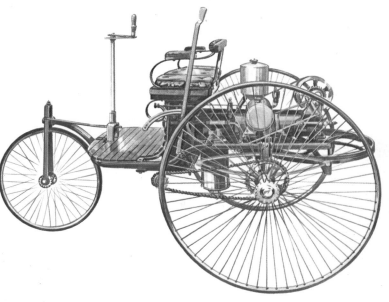

Röntgen—discoverer of X-rays

▼ Conrad Röntgen (1843-1923) discovered X-rays by accident, but soon saw the value of being able to study the inner structure of the human body. Before that, doctors had far less to guide them. He called them X-rays because he did not understand how they worked.

A new direction in air travel

► The zeppelin, named after Count Zeppelin, was the first successful rigid airship. The balloon which preceeded it could not be directed. Zeppelin arranged a number of balloons inside an aluminium frame covered with fabric, and fixed a motor. His airship made its first successful flight in 1900. After the First World War, interest in the zeppelin revived and the Graf Zeppelin (named after the Count) made many successful journeys. The weakness was that the gas-bags were filled with hydrogen, and on one trip to the United States the Graf Zeppelin caught fire and was destroyed. Recently people have been thinking again about ways in which giant airships could be used to carry goods.

Products of quality and precision

A wide choice of food

Delicatessen shops can be found in big towns in many parts of the world. These have been copied from Germany, and the best are still to be found there. There one can see dozens of different kinds of sausage, smoked pork and salmon, hams and herrings in a variety of different styles and prepared dishes made of game and wild fowl. Dozens of different German cheeses named after districts as well as a mouth-watering variety of sandwich-spreads are found. By buying small quantities of lots of different things Germans can make a delicious supper or picnic-meal. Real German food-products, such as pretzels, pumpernickel, sauerkraut and frankfurter sausages sell well abroad, in spite of imitations and lower prices.

Germany produces less wine than France. It is different in type, but is also very famous and sells for high prices. Although the right wine enhances food, Germans often prefer to drink their equally famous beer at meal-time, and drink wine when friends call, or when they go out to the cafe.

Quality manufacture

Germans have established a great reputation for the finish of their goods and the care which is put into their manufacture. In this way, they have become famous for their cameras and scientific instruments, where careful work is necessary to produce perfect results.

The same careful work, good design and continuous improvement have made West Germany famous for its motor cars. There have been many clever inventors among German engineers. In recent years the Wankel car-engine, which has fewer moving parts, has attracted interest, although most car manufacturers have still to be convinced that it will take the place of the ordinary engine.

Volkswagen—the great success story

The Volkswagen was designed in the 1930s as a car for everyman, but few were built. The factory was damaged during the war, but, with British help, German workers built 1,800 cars by the end of 1945. Production now exceeds 10,000 vehicles a day.

Volkswagen statistics

Car production		
	1945	1,800 cars
	1947	8,987
	1951	100,000
	1971	2,350,000

Total sales are over 23,400,000 cars.

▼ The "beetle" is the best-known of the VW cars. Improvements are constantly made, but the latest Volkswagen is very similar in its appearance to the first model made nearly forty years ago.

▼ Interior of a German car assembly plant. At Wolfsburg, Volkswagen has the largest plant, housed under one roof, to be found anywhere in the world.

◀ The chemical industry is second only to mechanical engineering in importance in West Germany. The names of the leading firms are known all over the world.

▼ Germany has long been famous for its cameras and similar precision work. The famous firm of Carl Zeiss moved to West Germany at the end of the war.

▼ Germany has always been world-famous for its porcelain. The best-known varieties, Dresden and Meissen, come from areas now in East Germany. But the Nymphenburg factory, of which the Dukes of Bavaria were patrons, is near Munich. Since the war, some new West German firms have achieved international importance. Stoneware, which has long been a speciality of the Rhineland, is also important.

▼ A modern rolling-mill for producing steel plate. Krupp is one of the best-known names in heavy engineering. It once produced much of the war material which made Germany a powerful military nation.

◀ German wines are famous and their quality is strictly controlled. Most German wines are white, and come from eleven major wine-growing districts, mostly along the Rhine and Moselle. Every year, before the harvest, the vats are emptied, to make room for the new wine, and villages in the area hold wine festivals.

Getting about in West Germany

▲ The great Rhine barges carry many of the raw materials upon which the factories of West Germany depend. The barges have powerful engines to go against the current.

▼ A Hanover street scene. Unlike many other countries which have done away with trams, West Germany still makes considerable use of them.

Autobahns and waterways

West Germany has the busiest transport system in the world. Over ten times as many cars pass over a mile of road in Germany as do in France.

Germany was the first European country to build a modern system of motorways. These have been much extended and improved, and it is possible now to travel quickly and comfortably from one end of the country to the other. Even so, the road system is now stretched almost to its limits. West Germany is, therefore, fortunate in also having a very good system of air, rail, and river transport. The waterways system is based on the great river Rhine, and a series of canals. One trip not to be missed is a journey by Rhine steamer along the most interesting part between Cologne and Mainz.

The variety of transport

Although many countries have given up trams, many German cities still find them useful. They usually consist of two coaches, linked together.

In out-of-the-way places, and in the mountains, the Post Office runs small yellow-painted coaches, which carry passengers as well as letters.

West Germany is working on ideas for extra-fast trains, but already its *Trans-Europe Express* (T.E.E.) trains are among the best in the world.

Lufthansa—the German airline

▲ A "spaghetti junction" on a Berlin *autobahn*. The motorways of West Germany are among the most up-to-date in Europe. There were 4,460 km (2,770 miles) of motorway in 1970 and a further 1,800 km (1,120 miles) are to be built by 1975.

The West German motor industry

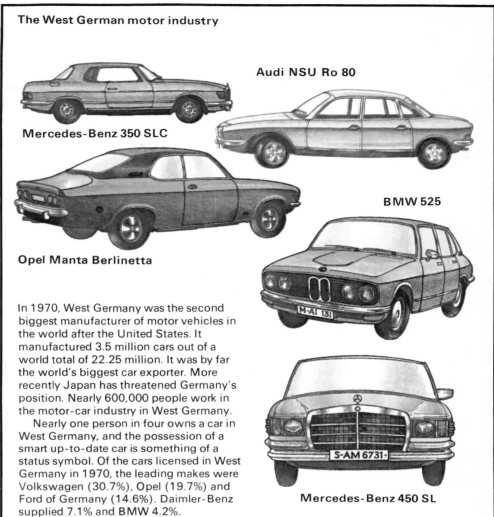

Mercedes-Benz 350 SLC

Audi NSU Ro 80

Opel Manta Berlinetta

BMW 525

Mercedes-Benz 450 SL

In 1970, West Germany was the second biggest manufacturer of motor vehicles in the world after the United States. It manufactured 3.5 million cars out of a world total of 22.25 million. It was by far the world's biggest car exporter. More recently Japan has threatened Germany's position. Nearly 600,000 people work in the motor-car industry in West Germany.

Nearly one person in four owns a car in West Germany, and the possession of a smart up-to-date car is something of a status symbol. Of the cars licensed in West Germany in 1970, the leading makes were Volkswagen (30.7%), Opel (19.7%) and Ford of Germany (14.6%). Daimler-Benz supplied 7.1% and BMW 4.2%.

▼ A Lufthansa plane. Since 1954, when the present corporation was formed, the West German national airline has become the fifth biggest carrier, with services to every continent. In 1971, it carried $7\frac{1}{2}$ million passengers. In recent years, the volume of business has increased well above world average. Most of its planes are Boeing jets.

▲ A new suburban station on the outskirts of Munich. The city prides itself on its very modern integrated service of bus, tram and underground transport.

Munich
city of festivals

The beginnings of Munich

Munich is the capital of the state of Bavaria, and the third largest West German city.

For such an important place, its history is not a long one. Munich first became important about 1157 when Duke Henry the Lion destroyed the bridge belonging to the local bishop, and made the merchants pay a toll to cross his bridge, where Munich now stands. Later Munich was given the right to hold a market, and to mint coins. The salt trade made Munich rich and the town became an important trading centre. The local royal family decided to build a palace there. As Munich grew, architects, artists and musicians came to settle there.

Holidays and festivals

Today, Munich is important for cars, electrical goods and printing. The town is so busy that it employs many foreign workers, as well as workers from other parts of Germany.

Yet Munich still keeps its character. Religion is important and there are some fine churches. Schwabing, the artists' quarter, is very lively. No other German town has so many holidays, popular feasts and shows. The famous October festival, at harvest time, is an occasion for feasting, dressing up and fun. It is this enjoyment of life for its own sake which many people find so attractive about Munich.

What to see in Munich

Town Hall

Frauenkirche

Alte Pinakothek

English garden

Museum of art

Theatinerkirche

Bahnhof

Playhouse

Frauenkirche

National opera

Karlstor

Rathaus

Town Hall

Isartor

Sendlinger Tor

Hofgarten

Viktualienmarkt

Hall of Fame

Fasching

▲ A cafe in Munich. These cafes are excellent places to sit and talk, to read magazines, or play a game of chess.

▼ The Olympic Stadium, Munich. This stands on the northern outskirts of the town and was specially built for the 1972 Olympic Games. The Games, which were the most costly and most elaborate ever organized, attracted athletes from all over the world.

▲ The Nymphenburg Palace with its ornamental lake. This palace, which is a short bus ride from Munich, was the summer residence of the Kings of Bavaria. It was started in 1664, and took more than 100 years to build. Nearby is the famous Nymphenburg china factory.

▼ A view of Munich over the roof-tops. Munich is the capital of Bavaria and the biggest city in southern Germany. In the middle distance are the twin towers of the Frauenkirche, and on the far right is the television tower. The city, like so many in Germany, was badly damaged during the war. It has now been rebuilt.

▲ The Munich *Oktoberfest*. This takes place every autumn, and is an occasion for processions and wearing fancy dress.

The river Rhine the great artery

The world of the Rhine

The Rhine is the most important river in Europe. Many of Germany's most important industries stand on the river, or on its tributaries or canals, which are linked to the Rhine. As a result, much of the coal, oil, iron-ore and wood, which the factories need, and some of the finished articles, are carried by water.

Many families live their whole lives on barges with powerful engines, which travel up and down between Basle, on the Swiss border, and Rotterdam on the North Sea.

Between Mainz and Cologne, most of the factories are left behind, and the river flows through beautiful, hilly country. There are several small towns and villages. This part of the river is famous for its vineyards, planted on the sides of the hills.

Castles and legends

Along this part of the Rhine are a number of ruined castles on hill-tops. Knights and landlords, who owned the land along the river, made the traders pay tolls to pass by, and sometimes sent out raiding-parties to rob them. There are many legends about the most famous of these castles. Today some of the castles are used as cafes, restaurants, and youth hostels, and one near a dangerous stretch of the river serves as a signal station for shipping. Some castles can be bought for low prices, but the new owner must pay the cost of restoration, and preserve the original character.

In early times, parts of the Rhine were very dangerous, and many stories were told of daring adventures and miraculous escapes. The most famous is the legend of the Lorelei, who lived on a craggy rock which juts out into the river, and lured boatmen to their death by her singing.

▲ Cologne Cathedral is well known to visitors. It was begun in the middle ages but remained unfinished until 1880.

▲ Carnival time in Cologne. The man wearing the medal has won first prize for making funny speeches.

◄ The Pfalz stands in the middle of the Rhine near Kaub. The local landowner built it in 1326 to collect customs from merchants travelling by river. Prisoners were kept there in deep dungeons.

▲ The Benedictine abbey of Maria Laach near Koblenz. It was founded in 1093. After it had fallen into disrepair it was restored and now serves as a centre for the study of monastic history.

▲ Chair-lift at Assmannshausen. From here one can make excursions into the Niederwald and the Taunus.

▲ Inn at Bacharach. Such architecture can often be found in Rhineland villages and towns.

▲ A signal station opposite the Lorelei rock. Heine wrote a famous poem about the legend of the rock.

Frederick the Great of Prussia

Frederick the state builder

Frederick the Great (1712-86) made Prussia one of the two great states in Germany, and out of Frederick's powerful Prussia Otto von Bismarck later created the German Empire.

Frederick hated his father, who thought that Frederick was too fond of books and would never make a good soldier and king. At one time, Frederick even planned to run away from home. But when he became king, he became interested in the army.

Soon after he became king, Frederick saw that there were opportunities to make Prussia more powerful. The Emperor of Austria had died, and Maria Theresa became Empress. Other countries, including Prussia, had given a promise that she should be allowed to rule undisturbed. Frederick broke the promise, seizing the rich province of Silesia.

His plans for Prussia nearly went wrong in 1756, when he attacked Saxony. This time he was opposed by Austria, France and Russia. He was in danger of losing the war,

▲ Statue of Frederick the Great (1712-86). He is represented riding his favourite horse, a familiar sight during his lifetime. Although Frederick, as a young man, resented his father's attempts to make him into a good soldier, he later changed his mind about the importance of the army to the future greatness of his country. He frequently took personal charge on the battlefield.

▶ The Battle of Lowositz, October 1756. The battle, begun in fog, caused heavy losses to both Austrians and Prussians. Frederick's infantry, however, finally triumphed.

▼ Sans Souci Palace, near Berlin. Frederick had long rows of glass-houses built on the terraced slopes. Here he grew the flowers he loved.

and was only saved because the Empress of Russia died. Her son, the new Emperor, was a great admirer of Frederick.

Frederick had still one more ambition. He wanted to split up the weak Kingdom of Poland. In 1772, he persuaded Russia and Austria to join him in sharing out the country among themselves.

Frederick's character

Frederick was a curious mass of contradictions. He considered himself the servant of the Prussian state, but he despised the German language and his subjects, who, he thought, were boorish. He had the greatest admiration for everything French. He had liberal ideas about government, but he ruled his country like a dictator. He made Prussia rich and powerful and earned the title Frederick "the Great". Yet if he had been defeated earlier in his career (as could easily have happened) he would have been known as an ambitious failure. When he died, at 74, a bitter and exhausted man, the people of Prussia rejoiced.

▲ Jena University at the time of Frederick the Great. The king was a great patron of the arts. He admired learning, and scholarship benefited during his reign.

▶ Johann Sebastian Bach (1685-1750). He was the most famous of a distinguished family of composers. He frequently visited Frederick at Sans Souci, and composed some chamber music under the patronage of the king.

▲ Voltaire reading his work to Frederick. The king admired French culture, and became a friend of the French philosopher.

Frederick often invited famous thinkers and artists to his palace. Voltaire went to live at Sans Souci, but later the two quarrelled.

Otto von Bismarck the Iron Chancellor

Bismarck's early career

Count Otto von Bismark (1815–98) did more than anybody to create a united Germany. His methods were often harsh, and he often went directly for what he wanted, without bothering about his methods.

He came from a Prussian land-owning family, and at first was not much interested in politics. He later became a strong supporter of the king and of the Prussian army. He also saw that if Germany was to become important she must be united.

He was elected to the Parliament in Frankfurt in 1848. His position, however, was difficult, because he disliked the liberal ideas of many of the members. He also wanted Austria to be left out of the new Germany he hoped to create.

The master strategist

When he became Prime Minister of Prussia in 1862, he set about strengthening the army. He also took steps to make friends with Russia so that he would not have to fight on two fronts at once if war broke out. He also decided to follow two rules—never to fight a day longer than necessary in getting what he wanted, and also, if possible, to make his opponent take the first step. Even so, it was not easy to persuade the king and parliament to support his policy of "blood and iron". In 1864, Prussia and Austria quarrelled with Denmark about two provinces. The Danes were quickly beaten. Two years later he provoked Austria into declaring war. Austria, too, was beaten, but Bismarck was generous over the peace settlement. As a result, when France was tricked into declaring war, Austria did not come to France's aid.

France, too, was soundly beaten. After the peace, the King of Prussia was declared Emperor of Germany in January 1871 in the Palace of Versailles.

Bismarck had achieved his ambitions, but he had no sympathy with the wild schemes of the new Emperor, who succeeded his late master. In 1890 he resigned, and spent the rest of his life in retirement.

▲ Count von Bismark (1815-98). He was the statesman mainly responsible for unifying Germany. He became the first chancellor.

▼ Proclamation of William I as the first emperor of Germany. The ceremony took place in the Hall of Mirrors at Versailles after the defeat of France, in 1871.

▲ The siege of Mont Valerien, Paris, January 1871. After the defeat of the French at Sedan, the German army closed in on Paris. The war ended with the surrender of these forts.

▼ Bismarck manipulated the Emperors of Germany, Russia and Austria as if they were puppets. The *Punch* cartoon of the period illustrates Bismarck's great power.

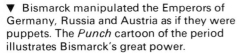

▲ The Congress of Berlin, 1878. Bismarck called a conference of leading statesmen to solve the problems of eastern Europe.

▼ 'Dropping the pilot'. This famous cartoon by Tenniel appeared in *Punch* after the new German emperor William II had forced Bismark from office.

▲ William II, Emperor of Germany (1888-1918). He alarmed Britain and France by his aggressive policies. Bismarck had been no less active, but William II lacked Bismarck's skill.

An era of war and defeat

▶ German troops surrender to the British during World War I. The fighting had become a stalemate.

▼ Statesmen of the victorious powers at Versailles, in 1919, for the peace negotiations. The peace treaty was signed in the same Palace where the German Empire had been proclaimed in 1871.

▲ Hitler with his earliest supporters. His first attempt to seize power in 1923 failed. While in prison he wrote *Mein Kampf* in which he set out his political ideas.

▲ Hitler in the 1930s. He was at the height of his power. After Hindenburg's death in 1934, Hitler became absolute ruler of Germany.

Kaiser William II

In 1888, Germany had three emperors in quick succession. The old emperor and his son died within a few months of each other. The new emperor, William II, was only 29. He not only lacked experience, he was restless, ambitious and vain. He was not satisfied with the progress which Germany had made. He wanted to be as great, or greater than anybody else. Although Germany did not need them, he wanted colonies, and a great navy to match the great German army. These plans, and the tactless way the Kaiser behaved, thoroughly alarmed Britain and France. This helped lead to the First World War, the most terrible war in history.

After the defeat of Germany and the abdication of the Kaiser, a republic with more liberal ideas was created. These were very hard years for Germany, but to make things worse, conditions became bad all over the world. Germany could not make progress in spite of her efforts.

These were ideal conditions for extremists. Both the Communists, and their enemies the Nazis, made progress, but in the end the Nazis were elected to power, and Hitler became leader of the German people. All opposition was stamped out. Hitler built up, first secretly and then openly, the armed forces.

The Second World War

Although they wished to avoid war, the great powers became alarmed when Germany seized not only small areas along her borders where German-speaking populations lived, but whole countries, such as Austria and Czecho-Slovakia. War broke out again in September 1939 after Germany attacked Poland, and eventually nearly the whole world became involved. At first, Germany was very successful though outnumbered, but eventually the United States joined the allies. In 1945, Germany was invaded and forced to surrender.

It was not easy to find a form of government for Germany, since Russia and her supporters wanted one thing, and the western allies another. At last it was agreed that until a Peace Treaty was signed Germany would be governed as two separate states. Even Berlin, which lies inside East German territory, is divided into two.

The Federal Republic of Germany has been an independent state since 1955. Although many West Germans ask themselves when East and West will be re-united, many are content to leave things as they are.

▲ Liberation of Paris, August 1944. The German forces were led away into captivity. The Paris garrison offered little resistance after the allies had broken through into France following the Normandy landings.

▶ The partition of Germany. Russia had advanced into Germany from the east while the other allies moved in from south and west. The partition roughly represents the areas occupied by each. Berlin in the East is divided neatly in two.

◀ German tanks advancing into Russia. After invading in June, 1941, the Germans advanced rapidly; even the beginning of the severe Russian winter a few months later did not seem to threaten them.

▼ Defeated Germany, June 1945. After the defeat food and fuel were very scarce. Buildings, roads, railways and equipment had been destroyed. People were obliged to raid the refuse lorries for what they could find.

Germany after World War II

Hamburg

Berlin

EAST GERMANY

Bonn

WEST GERMANY

▶ A
This
of th
boo
fore
play
Emil
chilc
This
Emil'
orgai
justic

▲ The Brandenburg Gate, Berlin. In front of the Gate is the Berlin wall, which cuts the city into two parts. It was erected by the East German government to prevent the escape of refugees to the West.

The West German character

▼ In every country, people have views about their national characteristics. However wrong, or overgeneralized, these notions might be, they do indicate the qualities people admire, and those they laugh at, in themselves. In Germany differences between the regions are considerable, but there are still qualities Germans believe are especially theirs.

How Germans see themselves

Perfectionists

Since the war, West Germans have had to review many of the ideas which they had come to accept. But although West Germany is as free and democratic as any country in the West, Germans emphasize different qualities.

Germans have always valued cleanliness and good order. To describe somebody as an orderly person is high praise, if somewhat patronizing. Germans appreciate a job well done, and many will go to enormous pains to achieve a perfect result. Sometimes, in the process, the job becomes more important than the product, with too much paper-work and "red tape". Germans would recognize, too, that they are not as good as some people at thinking for themselves, and altering plans to meet changing needs.

▲ Germans attach great importance to good order and efficiency. But time-consuming methods do not always pay.

Respect for authority

Some old ideas die hard. Older Germans still have great respect for authority. The police, especially, have done their best to create the image of "the policeman, your friend and helper", but they have not entirely succeeded. Although a suspect is innocent until he is proved guilty, there are still too many Germans who will say—especially if they feel strongly about a case—"he must prove his innocence". Although Germans are very kind and friendly to foreigners, the German idea that you must be made to learn by your mistakes can be very inconvenient if you are driving in the wrong traffic lane and people are unwilling to give way.

Germans are often sentimental people, which they cover up with a rugged exterior. Many of the best-loved traditional songs deal with the homesickness of the wanderer.

In Germany, companionship and good cheer are given more expression than in most countries. People enjoy each other's company, whether wandering about the countryside in groups or talking and singing together. But equally well, fellowship means the pleasure of good food and drink, consumed in pleasant surroundings. It is not surprising that the government has to warn people of the importance of keeping their weight down!

▲ Germans still have great respect for titles and authority, but younger people are noticeably less respectful!

▲ Most Germans would claim that they know how to enjoy themselves. Sometimes the fun is rather boisterous.

▲ Germans see themselves as fresh-air fiends. They love to get away from the city, and out into the sun.

▲ Germans are often great sentimentalists. Many of the best-known national songs deal with the sadness of being far from home.

▼ 'The policeman's job offers the young man with ideals a welcome opportunity to serve the community.' A cartoonist pokes gentle fun at old notions of an authoritarian police.

▲ Civic pride. Since Germany was slow to unite, local ties have always been strong, and people take great pride in their own town.

▼ "The sky is hung with violins" sing two lovers in an operetta. Germany has always produced fine instruments, and these, in a violin-making school, continue the tradition.

▲ A street in Bernkastel. In spite of rapid rebuilding in West Germany, the country still retains many of its old towns with their gaily decorated houses and quaint alleys. This village atmosphere is a source of pride to German people.

The changing face of West Germany

Rebuilding a nation

The disastrous defeat of Germany in 1945 meant that the West Germans had to rebuild homes and factories and to find jobs for the population and the millions of refugees who crowded in. Then they had also to create a new way of life.

West Germany has been very successful in doing many of these things. She has been particularly successful in building up industries. As a result, it has been necessary to bring in foreign workers from the Mediterranean countries and Turkey. Every third person at work now, too, is a woman. This is an important change from the days when Germans thought a woman's place was in the home.

Another change has been that millions of people have given up working on the land to work in the towns. Farms have been grouped together, and more machinery is used. Success has meant that German workers are paid higher wages, and hours of work have fallen. Today, the German is better off than any other European worker, in spite of the fact that prices are high and continue to rise.

A new way of life

One benefit which the war has brought to the West Germans is that they are now free to think and write without government interference. During the Nazi regime many German writers who dared to criticize society were imprisoned.

German parents are strict, and insist that their children are obedient and polite. Nonetheless young people seem to have more liberty now. German students, too, have ideas of their own about dress and behaviour, and about the way the world is run. They have been very ready to adopt ideas—including pop music—from Britain, America and France. They have made themselves heard in political matters, protesting against many forms of injustice. The old dreams of world domination have now been entirely forgotten.

The great leap in prosperity

	1949	1970
1 kilogramme of bread	23mins	13mins
1 kilogramme of sugar	58mins	11mins
1 kilogramme of potatos	37mins	18mins
1 kilogramme of pork chops	275mins	80mins
1 kilogramme of butter	253mins	71mins
1 kilogramme of coffee	1,357mins	161mins
1 shirt	12hrs	3hrs
1 Volkswagen	3,946hrs	787hrs

▲ The amount of working time it takes to buy various articles is a good measure of a country's prosperity.

▼ Factory chimneys near Düsseldorf. The *Land* (State) of North Rhine-Westphalia, where many of the big factories are, has taken a lead in stopping smoke pollution, but a great deal still needs to be done.

▼ Italian migrant workers buy provisions. Workers from poorer countries were brought in to relieve labour shortages after 1950 when German industry expanded rapidly. Today there are over two million of these 'guest-workers'.

▲ Student revolts occurred in Berlin and other university towns in 1968. They had many causes, and showed a general dissatisfaction with the state of society.

◄ West Germany has become a world leader in heavy engineering products.

▼ Helmut Schmidt, now one of the world's great leaders, became chancellor of the Federal Republic in 1974, after Willi Brandt resigned. He had previously held the important posts of Minister of Defence and of Finance.

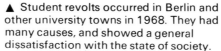

Reference
Physical and Human Geography

Land and people

Full title: Bundesrepublik Deutschland (Federal Republic of Germany)

Position: Between 6 and 14 E and 47 30 and 55 N. Occupying central position between Denmark and Switzerland, and between France and Soviet bloc to east. W. Germany has frontiers with nine other countries

Flag: Black, red, gold (horizontal stripes)

Anthem: *Einigkeit, und Recht, und Freiheit* (words by H. Hoffmann, 1841: tune by Haydn, 1797)

Constituent parts: The republic, comprising ten states (*Länder*) and West Berlin (a *Land* of the Republic, but not yet formally incorporated)

Area: 248,593 sq. km. (95,982 sq. miles), of which W. Berlin has 480 sq. km. (185 sq. miles)

Population: 1971 estimate 61,502,500: of which W. Berlin has 2,084,000

Capital: Bonn (pop. 280,000)

Language: German

Religion: Almost equally divided between Protestants (49%) and Catholics (44.6%). 0.005% are Jewish.

The state: The Basic Law of the Federal Republic was signed on May 23, 1949. It created a republican democratic state, based on the rule of law. It is provisional in so far that, if Germany is ever reunified, the entire German people would have to approve it.

Political System: Parliamentary democracy, based on system of direct, universal elections, and guaranteed by Basic Law of the constitution.

Armed Forces: Total, 467,500: army 326,700, incl. territorial army; navy, 36,700; air force, 104,100. About half of the strength of the armed forces is made up of men liable for basic service of 15 months. The U.S.A. and U.K. maintain defence forces at bases in West Germany.

International Organizations: West Germany was admitted as a member of the United Nations in September 1973. She has long been an active member of several of its special agencies. West Germany is also a member of the European Common Market, of O.E.C.D. and N.A.T.O.

The climate of West Germany

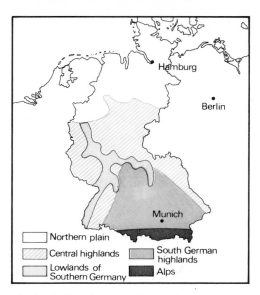

Northern plain

Central highlands

Lowlands of Southern Germany

South German highlands

Alps

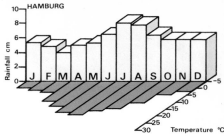

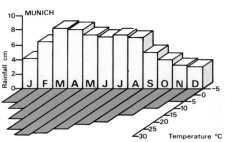

Much of West Germany has a climate not unlike England or the north coast of France, although winters are colder. The highest peaks of the Alps and the southern German high-lands are snow-covered from January to March; the highest summer temperatures are reached in the sheltered lowlands. The mean temperature throughout the year is about 9°c.

Natural vegetation in West Germany

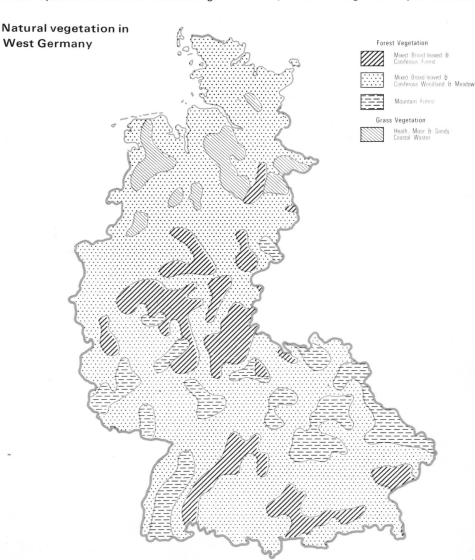

Forest Vegetation

Mixed Broad-leaved & Coniferous Forest

Mixed Broad-leaved & Coniferous Woodland & Meadow

Mountain Forest

Grass Vegetation

Heath, Moor & Sandy Coastal Wastes

The density of population

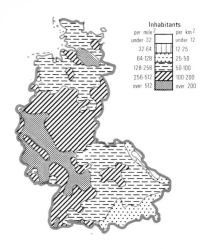

Inhabitants

per mile²		per km²
under 32		under 12
32-64		12-25
64-128		25-50
128-256		50-100
256-512		100-200
over 512		over 200

In spite of wartime losses, the population of West Germany has grown from 43 million to over 61 million in not much more than 25 years. This has partly been due to the influx of refugees from the east. In addition, there are about 2·5 million foreign "guest-workers", attracted by the chance of better jobs. As a result, the population is nearly three times as dense as that of France.

There are only three towns (including West Berlin) with populations over a million, but 60% of the population live in closely packed urban areas (*Ballungsgebiete*), such as Rhine-Ruhr or Frankfurt-Main. Germany has built some new towns, but, generally, redevelopment has been in already established urban areas.

Populations of principal cities

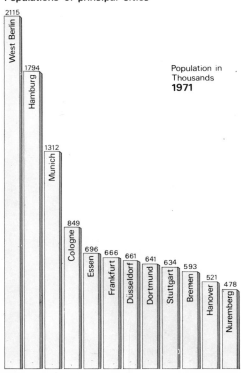

Population in Thousands
1971

City	Population
West Berlin	2115
Hamburg	1794
Munich	1312
Cologne	849
Essen	696
Frankfurt	666
Düsseldorf	661
Dortmund	641
Stuttgart	634
Bremen	593
Hanover	521
Nuremberg	478

Government

Federal President

Bundestag

Bundesrat

Federal Convention

Federal Chancellor

Federal Ministers

The Länder of the Federal Republic

The electorate

The Supreme Courts of the Federation

The political system of West Germany

After the defeat of 1945, Germany was divided into four zones, under British, American, French and Russian administration. The British and American zones were united for economic purposes in 1947. The French zone merged with them in 1948. Out of this the future state of West Germany was to grow.

In May 1949, the governments of Britain, the United States and France approved a so-called Basic Law, which the Germans had drawn up, and which gave the western half of Germany a federal form of government. This constitution, which had much in common with that of the U.S., allowed the German *Länder* (or states) wide powers, while reserving some important matters for the central federal government. It was not until May 1955 that the federal government became a sovereign state. The former occupying powers have retained the right to decide on the future of Berlin, the question of a possible re-unification of Germany, and the negotiation of a peace treaty.

The head of the Federal Republic is the President, but effective power is in the hands of the Federal chancellor (or prime minister), who leads the group which has a majority in the *Bundestag* (parliament). Each of the state governments has its own *Minister-Präsident* with his own cabinet.

West Berlin, which is surrounded by the East German state, is under the authority of the three Western allies. It sends non-voting representatives to the Federal Parliament, at Bonn.

Reference
History

MAIN EVENTS IN GERMAN HISTORY

B.C.

1000-100	Germanic tribes settle in north and central Europe.
58	Roman legions reach Rhine.

A.D.

9	Hermann's victory halts Roman advance beyond Rhine.
83	Defences on Rhine and Danube to keep out German tribes.
c. 370	Mass Germanic invasions begin.
401	Romans withdraw from Rhine.
481-511	Reign of Clovis.
768-814	Charlemagne creates great Frankish kingdom.
800	Charlemagne crowned emperor.
843	Empire divided: eastern part to Louis the German.
1056-1105	Henry IV. Struggle of emperor and Pope for supremacy.
1152-1190	Frederick Barbarossa. Conquers Slavs of E. Germany. Empire reaches greatest extent. Colonization of E. Europe starts. Rhineland cities and Hansa towns become more powerful.
1356	Golden Bull. German emperors to be elected at Frankfurt.
c. 1400	Reformation movement in Bohemia.
1517	Luther nails his "theses" on church door. Beginning of Protestant Reformation.
1521	Diet of Worms orders Luther's arrest.
1547	Victory of emperor over Protestant states.
1555	Peace of Augsburg. Subjects to adopt religion of their ruler.
1618-48	Thirty Years War.
1701	Kingdom of Prussia proclaimed.
1713-40	Frederick William I of Prussia.
1740-86	Frederick II, the Great, of Prussia.
1740	Frederick II invades Silesia.
1756-63	Seven Years War.
1792	Wars against Revolutionary France begin.
1803-15	Napoleonic Wars.
1806	Holy Roman Empire dissolved.
1813-15	War of Liberation under Prussia.
1815	Battle of Waterloo.
1814-15	Congress of Vienna. Prussia acquires Rhineland.
1815	German Confederation, including Prussia and Austria.
1848	Revolution in Germany: attempt to create a nation state.
1862	Bismarck becomes prime minister.
1864	Austro-Prussian victory over Denmark.
1866	Prussia defeats Austria.
1866-7	North German confederation.
1870	France declares war.
1871	German Empire proclaimed after defeat of France.

1872	Triple alliance of Germany, Austria and Russia.
1882	Triple alliance of Germany, Austria and Italy. Treaty with Russia not renewed in 1890.
1888-1918	William II emperor of Germany.
1890	Bismarck ousted.
1914-18	World War I, Germany defeated.
1918	Proclamation of republic.
1919-34	Weimar republic in Germany.
1922-3	Inflation in Germany.
1923	Hitler's Munich *Putsch.*
1925-34	Hindenburg German president.
1929	World economic crisis.
1933-45	Nazi party in power.
1933	Hitler becomes chancellor: Reichstag fire: other parties banned.
1938	Germany annexes Austria. Munich agreement on Czecho-Slovakia.
1939	Russo-German non-aggression pact. World War II follows attack on Poland.
1945	Unconditional surrender of Germany.
1948	Currency reform marks beginning of German recovery.
1948-9	Berlin crisis.
1949	Federal Republic of Germany and German Democratic Republic created from Western zones and Russian zone respectively. Adenauer first chancellor.
1953	Uprising in East Germany.
1955	N.A.T.O. admits W. Germany.
1957	W. Germany joins Common Market.
1961	Berlin wall built.
1963-6	Ehrhardt chancellor: period of "economic miracle"
1969	Brandt chancellor.
1970	Treaties signed with Poland and Russia.
1971	Four-part settlement on Berlin signed.
1972	Treaty with East Germany signed.

MARTIN LUTHER (1483-1546)

Son of free peasant family; studied at cathedral school and university of Erfurt. His father wanted him to become a lawyer.

1505 July	Abandons law and becomes a monk.
1510	Sent to Rome: horrified at lax behaviour of clergy there.
1512	Becomes professor at Wittenburg university. Began detailed study of Bible. Opposed the selling of Indulgences for the pardon of sins.
1517 Oct.	Nailed his 95 Theses to church door. Wanted the Church to reform itself from within.
1519 July	Debate with Johann Eck. Luther obliged to recognize that his ideas differed from the orthodox teaching of the Church.

1520 June	Pope's letter of excommunication. Luther burned the letter in public.
1521	Council of Worms: Luther outlawed. Protected by ruler of Saxony: translated Bible while in Wartburg castle.
1522	Returned to Wittenburg. Introduced services in German.
1524	Peasants rebel, demanding religious freedom and abolition of serfdom. Luther denounces them.
1525	Luther marries Katherina von Bara, a former nun.
1532	Lutherans allowed religious freedom.

UNIFICATION

1740	Frederick II of Prussia annexes Silesia.
1785	League of German Princes under leadership of Prussia.
1814-15	Congress of Vienna. Prussia acquires territories in Rhineland: Austria shifts its influence towards east.
1815	German Confederation founded.
1834	Customs union *(Zollverein)* established to encourage trade between German states.
1848-9	Attempt to revive German empire as a nation state.
1848 May	Frankfurt National Assembly called. Schleswig and Holstein revolt against their Danish ruler with support of Frankfurt. London Protocol (1852) restores territories to Denmark.
1849	Frankfurt constitution. Federal state under emperor of the Germans to be created.
March April	Throne offered to king of Prussia. Offer rejected.
June	Frankfurt assembly dissolved without creating parliamentary government for united Germany.
1849-50	Prussia and Austria propose rival systems for unifying Germany. Old German Confederation revived when these fail.
1853	All German states, apart from those in the Austrian empire, finally join *Zollverein* (customs union).
1864	Austro-Prussian victory over Denmark; Schleswig-Holstein passed under joint rule of Austria and Prussia.
1866	Seven Weeks' War. Prussia soundly defeats Austria.
1867	North German Confederation under leadership of Prussia. Bismarck becomes chancellor.
1870 July Sept.	France declares war on Prussia. France capitulates after defeat at Sedan.
1871 Jan.	Foundation of German empire. William I proclaimed emperor of Germany.

THE KAISER AND WORLD WAR I

1888	Kaiser Wilhelm II succeeds.
1890	Bismarck dismissed.
1896	Crisis with Britain after Kaiser congratulates the Boers for opposing British in South Africa.
1904	Anglo-French *Entente*.
1905	Kaiser visits Tangier: crisis intended to test strength of *Entente*.
1911	German warship sent to Agadir: second Franco-German crisis over Morocco.
1914 June	Assassination of Austrian Archduke.
July	Austria declares war on Serbia. Germany declares war on Russia.
Aug.	Britain declares war on Germany. Germany advances rapidly through Belgium.
Sept.	German advance halted on the Marne.
Dec.	Long period of trench warfare begins.
1916 May	Battle of Jutland; inconclusive.
1917 April	U.S. declares war on Germany; turning point in war.
1918 Nov.	Germany seeks armistice: Kaiser abdicates.
1919 June	Treaty of Versailles.

RISE OF NAZIS AND WORLD WAR II

1919	Nazi party formed.
1923	Hitler attempts to seize power in Munich: imprisoned.
1933 Jan.	Hitler appointed chancellor.
Feb.	Reichstag fire: all civil liberties suspended.
July	All other political parties suppressed.
1936	German army re-occupies Rhineland.
1938 Mar.	Germany annexes Austria.
Sept.	Munich crisis.
1939 Mar.	Germany extends hold over Czechoslovakia.
Aug.	German-Russian non-aggression pact.
Sept.	Germany invades Poland; Britain and France declare war on Germany: Poland defeated.
1940 May	Germany invades Low Countries; French front broken.
June	Germans enter Paris. Armistice with France. British forces retreat from Dunkirk.
Aug.	Beginning of Battle of Britain.
June	Germany invades Russia.
Dec.	United States enters war.
1942 Aug.	Germans reach Stalingrad.
Nov.	Battle of El Alamein; Germans defeated in north Africa.
1943 Jan.	German withdrawal from Caucasus begins.
1944 June	Allied landings in Normandy.
Aug.	Allies enter Paris.
1945 April	Russian and U.S. troops meet on River Elbe in Germany.
April	Hitler commits suicide.
May	Unconditional surrender of Germany.

The arts

MUSIC

Bach, Johann Sebastian (1685-1750) most famous of family of musicians: church and orchestral music

Handel, George Frederick (1685-1759), composer of *The Messiah, Samson* and many other works

Beethoven, Ludwig von (1770-1827): a great master; symphonies and concertos

Weber, Carl Maria von (1786-1827) composer of *Der Freischütz*

Mendelssohn-Bartholdy, Felix (1809-47) oratorios, orchestral music

Wagner, Richard (1813-83), operatic composer; *Tristan and Isolde, Ring of the Nibelungen*

Brahms, Johannes (1833-97) one of great masters of classical music forms. Symphonies, concertos, etc.

Humperdinck, Engelbert (1854-1921), composer children's opera *Hänsel and Gretel* and other operas: incidental music, esp. to Shakespeare

Hindemith, Paul (1895-1963); operas, orchestral and chamber music

Weill, Kurt (1900-50); operas, orchestral music. Best known for music for *Threepenny Opera*

Stockhausen, Karlheinz (1928-) orchestral and piano compositions

LITERATURE

Von der Vogelweide, Walther (c. 1170-c. 1230); peak-time of the wandering musician and poet

Luther, Martin (1483-1546); translated Bible into German. Important influence on use of German language

Lessing, Gotthold Ephraim (1729-81); *Minna von Barnhelm* and other plays. First great modern German writer

Goethe, Johann Wolfgang von (1749-1832); *Faust* and other plays. The greatest of German poets

Schiller, Frederick (1759-1805); *Wilhelm Tell, Maria Stuart* and other plays

Kleist, Henrich von (1777-1811); poet dramatist and novelist

Heine, Heinrich (1797-1856) one of Germany's greatest lyric poets and satirists

Mörike, Eduard (1804-75); poet. Member of so-called Swabian School.

Mommsen, Theodor (1817-1903); historian. Nobel Prize winner

Marx, Karl (1818-1883); author of *Das Kapital*, has been called 'the father of Communism'

Rilke, Rainer Maria (1875-1926); most influential German poet of his period. *Duineser Elegien, Sonette an Orpheus*

Hauptmann, Gerhart (1862-1946); Dramatist. Did much to draw attention back to work of German authors

Kafka, Franz (1883-1924); novelist and story writer. *The Castle, The Trial* and other novels

Mann, Heinrich (1871-1950); novelist

Mann, Thomas (1875-1955); *Buddenbrooks, The Magic Mountain* and other novels. Nobel Prize winner

Brecht, Bertolt (1898-1956) dramatist and poet. *The Threepenny Opera* and other plays. One of the most controversial and influential figures of the modern European theatre

Böll, Heinrich (1917-) author and satirist. Among most important of contemporary writers. Nobel prize winner

Grass, Günter (1927-) Controversial poet, novelist and dramatist. Master of extravagant invention in writing

ART

Riemenschneider, Tilman (1460-1531) wood-carver; esp. altar-piece at Rothenburg

Holbein, Hans, the Elder (c. 1465-1524), painter and engraver; altar paintings in Munich and Augsburg

Dürer, Albrecht (1471-1528), painter and engraver

Cranach, Lucas, the Elder (1472-1553) one of the leading painters of the German Renaissance

Altdorfer, Albrecht (1480-1538); painter, engraver and architect

Holbein, Hans, the Younger (1497-1543) painter and designer. Visited England and drew portraits of many leading figures of period

Graff, Anton (1736-1813), portrait painter. Painted many of leading figures of his period

Friedrich, Casper (1774-1840) landscape painter and engraver

Runge, Philipp Otto (1777-1810) artist

Gropius, Walter (1883-1969) architect. Founded the Bauhaus in 1919, which had great influence on all aspects of European art and architecture

Marc, Franz (1880-1916) painter. One of leading figures in Blue Rider (expressionist) movement

Beckmann, Max (1884-1950) Expressionist painter

Baumeister, Willi (1889-1955) Abstract painter

PHILOSOPHY

Kant, Immanuel (1724-1804); *Critique of Pure Reason, On Everlasting Peace*

Hegel, Georg Wilhelm (1770-1831); *Encyclopedia of Philosophic Sciences*

Schopenhauer, Arthur (1788-1860); *On the Fourfold Root of the Principles of Sufficient Reason*. One of the first to appreciate culture of India

Lassalle, Ferdinand (1825-64); political philosopher. Concerned with organization of workers

Nietzche, Friedrich (1844-1900); *The Birth of Tragedy*. Enunciated much misunderstood idea of 'superman'

Spengler, Oswald (1880-1936); *The Decline of the West*

Reference
The Economy

Agriculture in West Germany

In 1945, at the end of the Second World War,
the industrial areas of West Germany were
devastated. The process was carried to the
limit, for the allies destroyed anything which
was likely to help Germany to make war
again. Then, much usable material was taken
to the East as war reparations. The position
remained extremely difficult because
German money had become virtually
worthless.

The so-called "miracle" of German recovery began in 1948 with the reform of the
currency. Recovery was helped by the
willingness of the Germans to work hard, the
plentiful supply of labour, and the help
which poured in, especially from the United
States. In time, the war damage was repaired,
new factories were built, and West Germany
emerged as the greatest industrial power in
Europe, with the strongest currency in
the world.

From 1968 to 1973 Germany experienced
a second prolonged boom. Exporting
activities were highly successful. As a result
many new jobs and wages have risen con-
siderably. A further result is that Germany has
difficulty in acquiring enough imports to
balance the exports. This causes a strain on
world trade.

What is owned compared with other countries (1971)

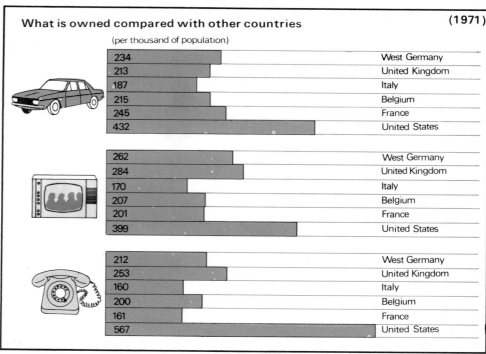

(per thousand of population)

Cars	
234	West Germany
213	United Kingdom
187	Italy
215	Belgium
245	France
432	United States

Televisions	
262	West Germany
284	United Kingdom
170	Italy
207	Belgium
201	France
399	United States

Telephones	
212	West Germany
253	United Kingdom
160	Italy
200	Belgium
161	France
567	United States

Industry in West Germany

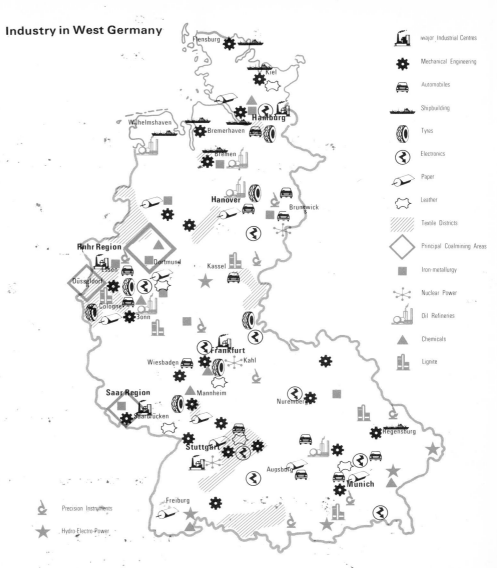

	Major Industrial Centres
	Mechanical Engineering
	Automobiles
	Shipbuilding
	Tyres
	Electronics
	Paper
	Leather
	Textile Districts
	Principal Coalmining Areas
	Iron-metallurgy
	Nuclear Power
	Oil Refineries
	Chemicals
	Lignite

Precision Instruments

Hydro-Electro-Power

West German Imports and Exports (1972)

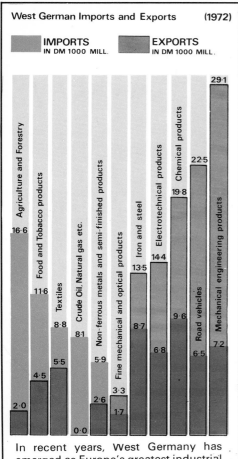

IMPORTS
IN DM 1000 MILL.

EXPORTS
IN DM 1000 MILL.

Agriculture and Forestry — 16·6 / 2·0

Food and Tobacco products — 11·6 / 4·5

Textiles — 8·8 / 5·5

Crude Oil, Natural gas etc. — 8·1 / 0·0

Non-ferrous metals and semi-finished products — 5·9 / 2·6

Fine mechanical and optical products — 3·3 / 1·7

Iron and steel — 13·5 / 8·7

Electrotechnical products — 14·4 / 6·8

Chemical products — 19·8 / 9·6

Road vehicles — 22·5 / 6·5

Mechanical engineering products — 29·1 / 7·2

In recent years, West Germany has emerged as Europe's greatest industrial power. One of her great difficulties has been to buy enough from abroad. Her exports have done so well that a great strain has been placed on the pattern of world trade.

The labour market

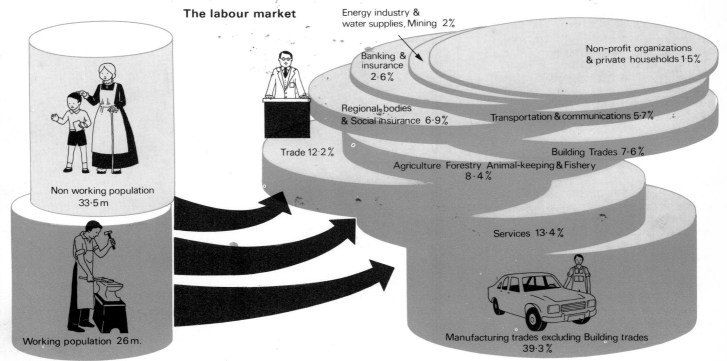

Non working population 33·5 m

Working population 26 m.

Energy industry & water supplies, Mining 2%

Banking & insurance 2·6%

Non-profit organizations & private households 1·5%

Regional bodies & Social insurance 6·9%

Transportation & communications 5·7%

Trade 12·2%

Building Trades 7·6%

Agriculture Forestry Animal-keeping & Fishery 8·4%

Services 13·4%

Manufacturing trades excluding Building trades 39·3%

59

Gazetteer

Aachen. (50 47N 6 5E) Important manufacturing town on *autobahn* from Cologne to Belgian border. Rich coal deposits. Burial-place and former residence of Charlemagne. Pop. 175,500.

Baden Baden. (48 56N 8 15E) Spa town south of Karlsruhe. Fine promenades and public gardens. Famous for its mineral springs since Roman times.

Bavaria. (49 5N 11 40E) Capital, Munich. A *Land* of the *Bundesrepublik*. Besides being important for agriculture and industry, it has some of the finest scenery in Germany. At one time an independent kingdom, it still retains some individual characteristics.

Bayreuth. (49 56N 11 35E) The town is world famous for its annual Wagner festival, which is held in the theatre designed by Richard Wagner himself.

Berlin, West. (52 34N 13 20E) Part of the old German capital, separated from East Berlin by the "Berlin wall". Under Four Power control, but associated for many purposes with the West German Republic. A highly important commercial and industrial centre. Pop. 2,115,000.

Bernkastel. (49 56N 7 05E) Famous Moselle wine town. It has many fine half-timbered houses. During the annual wine festival, wine flows from the fountain of St. Michael.

Bingen. (49 58N 7 57E) Port on north bank of Rhine at mouth of Nahe river. Tourist centre and centre of wine-growing area.

Black Forest. (48 20N 8 10E) Wooded, highly scenic area of 6,000 sq. km. (2,320 sq. miles) running parallel with Rhine and French Vosges. Famous tourist and winter sports centre. Important for wood carving and clock making.

Bonn. (50 43N 7 4E) Capital of Federal Republic of Germany. Formerly a quiet university and cathedral town 32 km (20 miles) south of Cologne. Birthplace of Beethoven. Pop. 280,000.

Bremen. (53 5N 8 43E) West Germany's second port, with important overseas trade, and distribution trade with Rhineland. Heavy wartime destruction of docks and commercial area now restored. Pop. 592,000.

Bremerhaven. (53 33N 8 35E) At mouth of Weser river, 33 miles north of Bremen. Biggest passenger, deep sea and coastal fishing port. Big shipyards. Pop. 143,000.

Brunswick. (52 15N 10 30E) A food-processing centre and Germany's leading sugar market. Industries include cars, machinery and factory equipment. Largely rebuilt since the war. Pop. 223,000.

Cologne. (50 56N 6 57E) Important Rhineland port and rail centre. One of great centres of German commerce, with some important industries. Famous cathedral. Starting point for many tourists in West Germany. Pop. 849,000.

Dortmund. (51 31N 7 27E) Important Ruhr town at head of Dortmund-Ems Canal. Famous for heavy industry and beer-brewing. Pop. 641,000.

Düsseldorf. (51 13N 6 47E) Rhineland city, capital of North-Rhine-Westphalia. The business centre of the Ruhr, with some important industries in suburbs. Its carnival attracts many visitors. Pop. 661,000.

Elbe, river. (54 0N 8 40E) One of Germany's most important rivers. Lower part forms boundary with East Germany. Linked to Rhine and Weser by canals. Flows through Hamburg to reach sea at Cuxhaven.

Essen. (51 26N 7 00E) Largest town in Ruhr coalfield. Great steel industry established here by Krupp family. Pop. 696,000.

Frankfurt am Main. (50 7N 8 40E) One of biggest and most dynamic trading centres in West Germany. Important trade fairs and motor show. Birthplace of Goethe. Pop. 666,000.

Freiburg im Breisgau. (48 0N 7 49E) Most important trading centre of Black Forest area. Contains many interesting old buildings and monuments. Pop. 164,000.

Hamburg. (43 24N 10 2E) West Germany's greatest port and second largest town. Harbour restored at cost of DM. 300 million after war. River Alster converted into fine boating lake. Pop. 1,794,000.

Heidelberg. (49 25N 8 40E) Attractive tourist centre on Main river. Lies between hills covered with vineyards and forests. Famous for its castle and university. Pop. 121,000.

Heligoland. (54 12N 7 52E) Island off North Sea coast of West Germany. Now bird sanctuary and holiday centre. British possession until 1890.

Karlsruhe. (49 3N 8 20E) Formerly a quiet provincial centre, named after Margrave Karl Wilhelm of Baden, who built castle there. Severely bombed in World War II. Pop. 259,000.

Kiel. (54 20N 10 10E) Gives name to canal which shortens journey from North Sea to Baltic. Excellent harbour, yachting centre. Pop. 271,000.

Koblenz. (50 20N 7 35E) Important tourist centre at junction of Rhine and Moselle rivers. One of largest mid-Rhine petroleum ports. One of oldest towns in Germany, but extensively rebuilt. Pop. 120,000.

Lübeck. (53 52N 10 40E) Important Baltic port and formerly chief city of Hanseatic League. Position undermined by construction of North Sea and Baltic Canal. Pop. 240,000.

Mannheim. (49 30N 8 26E) Second largest inland harbour in Europe. Highest navigable point for large ships on Rhine. Linked with Ludwigshaven by bridge. Pop. 332,000.

Mainz. (50 0N 8 15E) Provincial Rhineland capital and a centre of the wine trade. Gutenberg set up his first press here. This hand press and specimens of his work can be seen in the Gutenberg Museum. Pop. 175,000.

Mittenwald. (47 25N 11 20E) One of the most beautiful villages in the Bavarian Alps. Many fine walks and an important winter sports centre. Important for the manufacture of violins, which have been made here since the seventeenth century.

Moselle. (50 10N 7 20E) Tributary of Rhine, which it meets at Koblenz. Famous for vineyards which produce the Moselle wines.

Munich. (48 10N 11 36E) Capital of Bavaria. Third largest town of West Germany. Important industrial and cultural centre. Pop. 1,312,000.

Nuremberg. (49 30N 11 5E) Second largest city of Bavaria. Important manufacturing centre, but old city contains many interesting buildings. Former centre of Nazi rallies. Pop. 478,000.

Oberammergau. (47 35N 11 3E) World famous for its Passion Play, which the villagers have performed every ten years since 1634. The play lasts all day, with a break for lunch, and about 1,400 villagers take part.

Passau. (48 34N 13 27E) Stands where the rivers Danube, Inn and Ilz meet. This beautiful town is more than 2,000 years old. Among the interesting things to see is the world's largest church organ.

Rhine. The most important river in Europe. Flows about 500 km. (820 miles) from Swiss Alps to North Sea. It has been a great highway for trade between northern and southern Europe since prehistoric times.

Rüdesheim. (49 59N 7 55E) Town famous for its wines, and one of the most attractive of the places along the Rhine. Many houses dating from the middle ages.

Ruhr. (51 30N 8 0E) Largest single industrial area in world (about 5,000 sq. km. or 2,000 sq. miles). Principal towns, Essen, Dortmund, Duisburg, Gelsenkirchen and Bochum. Coal, iron and steel.

Saarbrücken. (49 17N 7 0E) Frontier town on French border. Industrial city in one of world's greatest coal-mining regions. Pop. 128,000.

Solingen. (51 10N 7 5E) Famous since middle ages for sword blades. One of chief centres for iron and steel industry: cutlery, razors, scissors, etc. Pop. 177,000.

Stuttgart. (48 50N 9 10E) Capital of *Land* of Baden-Wurttemberg. Largest industrial centre in south west Germany. Important book centre. Has oldest car factory in world. Pop. 634,000.

Taunus. (50 12N 8 10E) Wooded mountain range between Rhine and Main. Western border forms craggy peaks on which many Rhine castles have been built. Excellent walking country.

Trier. (49 45N 6 40E) Oldest town in Germany: many interesting Roman remains. Centre of Moselle wine trade. Pop. 104,000.

Wiesbaden. (50 6N 8 15E) One of oldest spa towns in Germany. Formerly a quiet provincial capital. Has now developed several industries. Famous for its *Sekt* (German champagne). Pop. 251,000.

Wuppertal. (51 15N 7 15E) Formed by grouping together several towns. Extends for 16 km., or 10 miles, along Wupper river, tributary of Rhine. World famous pharmaceutical and rubber companies. Unique monorail suspension railway. Pop. 418,000.

Index